DEATH
and
LIFE

Bianca Bowers

DEATH *and* LIFE
Copyright © 2018 by Bianca Bowers
Book Cover Design by Bianca Bowers

All rights reserved. No part of this publication may be reproduced, distributed, or transmitted in any form or by any means, including photocopying, recording, or other electronic or mechanical methods, without the prior written permission of the publisher, except in the case of brief quotations embodied in critical reviews and certain other noncommercial uses permitted by copyright law. For permission requests, email the publisher:
"Attention: Permissions"
info@paperfieldspress.com

www.paperfieldspress.com

Printed in Australia
ISBN-13: 978-0-9942404-9-1
eBook ISBN-13: 978-0-9942404-8-4

FIRST PUBLISHED IN 2014

POETRY BOOKS BY BIANCA BOWERS

Butterfly Voyage, 2018
Pressed Flowers, 2017
Love Is A Song She Sang From A Cage, 2016
Passage, 2015
Death and Life, 2014

Dedication

For those who struggle in their youth.

ACKNOWLEDGEMENTS

The Author thanks the following publications where these poems first appeared:-

The Wind, Tongue in Your Ear Volume 4 (Four/Two Publishing 1999)

His Sin, Tongue in Your Ear Volume 4 (Four/Two Publishing 1999)

Motherland, Spirits in Motion (The International Library of Poetry 2002)

Contents

THE STORY BEHIND DEATH AND LIFE	2
DEATH	5
Death and Life 1	6
I	7
The Road of Life	8
Smiling Bag	9
Blue Butterfly	11
Thief	12
Mortal Girl	13
Weekend	15
I Watched You Die	16
To Those I've Left Behind	18
Forgotten Garden	21
II	23
Eleven	24
Predators	25
Obsession	26
Hostage	24
His Sin	25
Help	26
III	31
The Absence of Happiness	32
Sadness	33
Bleed	34

Depression	35
Darkness	36
Thought Tunnel	37
The Mirror	38
Porcelain Ribs	39
Unlovable	41
Rain	44
IV	45
Vulnerable	46
The Wind	47
In Reality	48
If	50
Wasted	51
Loved and Lost	52
Unrequited Love List	53
Love Storm	55
Merlot Heart	57
Desire	58
V	61
Purpose	62
Death Star	63
Faceless	64
Sky	65
Dreams	66
Success	67
Yesterday	68
VI	69

Death Addiction	70
Amplified Silence	71
Perforated	72
Eclipse	75
4 Days Later	76
Insomnia	77
The Other Side	78
Answers	79
LIFE	81
Death and Life II	82
VII	83
Forfeit	84
Survival	86
Africa	87
Motherland	88
Leaving	89
Extradition	91
Migrant Skin	93
VIII	95
Winter Landscape	96
Shipwreck	97
Seek	98
Journey	99
The Path	101
The Ocean Heaves	102
To The Rocks	103
The Secret Bench	104

Seagull Party	105
The Night Moves	106
Self-Discovery	107
Searching	108
IX	109
Protector of my heart	110
The Kiss	111
Dance Me To The End Of Love	113
Love Garden	114
Liebe	116
X	119
Dream Cocoon	120
Mara	122
Jar of Secrets	124
Proposal	125
Goodbye Rangi	126
XI	127
The Forgotten Female	128
Freedom	132
Monarch	133
XII	135
Tree of Life	136
Purple Hibiscus	137
Anchors	138
Slumbering Queen	140
Life Swims	142

Sycamore Fig	144
The Death and Life of a Name	146
NOTES	149
ABOUT THE AUTHOR	152
A NOTE FROM THE AUTHOR	153
BOOK REVIEW GUIDE	154

The Story behind Death and Life

I lived with depression through my adolescence and early 20s, mostly due to abuse which was later compounded by an attack that disrupted and ended my first year of university. With my dreams crushed and no sense of direction, I spent the next three years venturing down many avenues without making it to the end of a single road. Adding to my vocational failures, I was failing on a personal level too. In addition to a destructive relationship that I seemed incapable of releasing myself from, I struggled to adapt to the increasingly violent landscape of post-apartheid South Africa. Somewhere along the line recreational substances crossed the border into an addictive coping mechanism as I attempted to desensitise myself to the violence and poverty that had fast become the accepted norm. When my parents immigrated without me, leaving a lot of loose ends, my decaying foundations crumbled and eventually resulted in my attempted suicide.

    I quickly realised that people had strong opinions about suicide and friends were not what they seemed. Most of my 'friends' dispersed like crowds in a bomb scare, and those who hung around seemed to do so out of a morbid fascination. When I talk about leaving South Africa with nothing but a suitcase, I mean that literally. When I moved to New Zealand, I started from scratch. In addition to having no money, I was a shell of a person and my only goal for the next 12 months was to make it through the day without falling apart and without the help of drugs or alcohol. With the help of numerous self-help books, physical exercise, and writing, I focused on my own personal development by undergoing tireless self-analysis and trying to change my negative behaviour patterns. For the next 15 years I never breathed a word about my suicide attempt, or my struggle with depression, or my past. After all, if my 'friends' who had known my circumstances had judged me, then I could only imagine what strangers were likely to do.

In retrospect, I was healing myself in one way but hurting myself in another. Continuing to live in the same manner of the past by being secretive about who I was and what had happened to me. In early 2013, I finally acknowledged that my authentic life would never be wholly realised until I was honest - regardless of judgement. That's when I decided to create my blog (bgbowers - no longer in existence) and publish my poetic confessions. It was liberating, to say the least, not to mention comforting when strangers began to reach out to me. It also unleashed the imagination, that I had once thought lost in childhood, and confirmed my unequivocal passion for writing.

Six months in I had no doubt that writing was my future, but it also dawned on me that most of my work was tied to the past - the old me - it was another person's voice and her story needed to be released. I believed for many years that I had an obligation to reach out to people and share my failures and flaws, anger and sadness, questions and answers, discoveries and rejections. Why an obligation? Because the act of sharing gives others permission to embrace their own truth and wear it like a badge of honour instead of hiding it in shame.

That's when Death and Life was born. I published Death and Life in March 2014, and, four years on, I still have mixed emotions about my decision to publish. Like a new home-owner suffers from buyers remorse, I have consistently suffered from publishers-remorse over this book. As a result, the book has been unavailable for purchase longer than it has been available . Some days I pick it up and tell myself that it's not so bad. Most days I turn it over, or hide it underneath another book, because I can't bear to look at it. I just want to press rewind and undo what I've done. It's all about judgement - judging my past and my writing.

    Four years down the line, me and my writing have come a long way, and I am finally content to allow this book to be. To accept that it contains my earliest writings - as far back as 1987, when I was still in primary school - and honour the young girl who wrote her darkest thoughts and kept these painful secrets until they overshadowed her.

DEATH

"Death is the great disruptor. It thrusts us opposite life's mirror, invites our truthful exploration, and reveals the naked truth, from which rebirth is possible and we are free to reinvent ourselves anew."

Death and Life I

Life
dictates Death.
Time is suspended, Mortality is certain
Puppets with strings, scissors poised
Destiny is inescapable, darkness devours light
Religion dictates judgement, sins are unforgettable
Eternity condemned, heaven or hell
Hearts fearing, souls burning
Nature is unnatural, pleasure is sinful
Guilt influences choice, Dogma breeds ethos
Happiness is impossible
Life and Death
~ condemning ~
Death and Life
Impossible is happiness
Dogma breed's ethos, Choice influences guilt
Sinful is pleasure, unnatural is nature
Burning souls, fearing hearts
Hell or heaven, condemned eternity
Unforgettable are sins, judgement dictates religion
Light devours darkness, inescapable is destiny
Poised scissors, strings with puppets
Certain is mortality, suspended is time
Death dictates
Life.

I

Death descended like a theatrical storm over the Drakensberg Mountains, stranding the living while it ran its course.

THE ROAD OF LIFE
For Chris

The road of life
dark and quiet
beneath my feet
before morning breaks
when the air is thick with fog;
Impenetrable
are we.
Street lights, few
and far between;
lit, fading, shrouded, blackout.
Intersections,
forks, turns, bypasses
criss, crossing
opening, closing
signposts missing
streets with no names...
The road of life
quietly lit beneath my feet
as morning breaks.

SMILING BAG

Here he comes
the man with the empty bag
your earthly name,
scribed in bold
across the black rubber of its lifeless skin, soon
the indifferent mist will hem your margins, soon
the carnation tinge, that kisses your mortal cheeks,
will turn;
anaemia, soon
Winter's snow will claim your hollow bones, soon
your humanity will be tamed beneath the zip
of a smiling bag.

Here he is
the man with the brimming bag
the weight of your mortality
decomposing
inside the lifeless rubber of its black skin
indifferent to the cold mist that hems your margins
carnations line parlour tables, and men's lapels
Winter's rigour mortis at its height
within your hollow bones
the weight of your humanity
housed beneath a timber frame.

There he goes
the man with the empty bag
the remains of your humanity,

a memory,
inside the black rubber of its slippery skin
the fugacious mist, evaporated
carnations sprout in the shadow of pale smiles
Winter retreats with changing conditions
your earthly name,
etched in italics
across the bones of marbled stone.

Blue Butterfly

I don't remember her name
It was too common to recall
But I remember who she was
A blue butterfly
Markings on her wings
like teardrops
There was mysterious sadness
in her moon-shaped eyes
A sadness that drew me
A sadness I strangely related to
A sadness that enveloped her
Her wings failed her
as she rested her chin
on the elephant barrel
The elephant and the butterfly
The blue too bruised to flutter
The teardrops too heavy to soar
And though she is gone
Time is powerless
to smudge her memory
Her blue wings at peace
in my heart

Thief

Time is powerless to subdue
the memory of that solitary night
when everything was wrong
beyond the strange window.

A secretive moon, intimidated by clouds.
A trespassing wind
surged up the willow-lined-driveway.
Red rain drops
scattered
upon the windowsill.

A shrill ring pierced the night.
Mother's wary footsteps descended stairs
quietly shivering in bed - I waited -
muffled sounds of loss ascended
like speech bubbles.
A thief broke and entered;
grief's shadow, the only trace.

MORTAL GIRL
For Nicole

She was loved by all
placed on pedestals
this mortal girl.
Her beauty lit the room
of father's heart
like mine never could.

Friday the 13th, 1989
lived up to its reputation
and distinguished her light.
We searched the long arms of night
waited for the darkness to blink
begged the moon to spill its secrets
but the silence of night was final.

The sunrise brought false hope
and little joy
as the Xerox worked overtime
and a lost smile
found it's way to every lamppost in Kloof
(but when have posters not been in vain?)
The police car in the driveway
and her best friend's expression
killed the last of my youthful hope
and that gorge of death, and ravine of tears
claimed my relationship with paternity.
So loved was this mortal girl

and so shocked was her congregation of followers
that men of God all hailed
their modern day resurrection.
Her funeral, a fever pitch
of frenzied faith
as the circus of fools
waited in vain
for this mortal girl
to rise from her coffin
but any hope of resurrection
was vetoed by her choice

The light of love followed her through the door
of no return
leaving me with broken pedestals, I could not fix
and a seed of doubt that grew into a new door
that tempted my entry, year,
after year, after year.

She was loved by all
this mortal girl
her beauty lit the room of father's heart
like mine never could.

Weekend
For Jane

The weekend promised fun for all
but she wasn't laughing
when his humour clipped her wings.

The weekend promised time for lovers
but an eternity
wasn't what they had in mind.

The weekend promised a party for friends
but a bottomless drink
ended the celebrations.

The weekend promised youthful freedom
but freedom from youth
was a step too far.

The weekend promised justice
but a paltry fine
was all he paid for taking her life.

I Watched You Die

I watched you die
under a baobab tree .
Your spirit rose and fell
like red dust on the dirt road.
Black cornrows
smiled, unnaturally
like a red gash across the sky.

Sobbing so intense
I couldn't catch my breath.
Palpitations descended,
as panic rose
from my toes to my head.

We held each other so tight ;
clinging desperately .
You slipped away,
life force
bleeding out.
My energy, sapped
like sticky syrup
from the blue gum tree.

Your last exhalations
clammy
on my moist cheeks.

A honeysuckle stopped to see.

Bianca Bowers

Her tiny body, hovered
over yours
momentarily.
And as her gentle wings
flapped
your eyes blinked
finality
and closed.

To Those I Have Left Behind

I know it's hard for you to understand
why I have chosen to leave you all behind.

You feel frustrated, because you think
if I had held on a little longer,
I would have made a turn
and seen a ray of light.
You feel guilty, because you didn't know,
you didn't see it coming.
You blame yourself for not trying hard enough,
not persevering one more time.
But most of all, you feel pain.
A void in your heart
in the space I used to fill.

I want you to know, it is not your fault.
The blame lies with no-one.
Feel blessed for the time you have had with me,
do not feel cheated for the time you have lost.
It is hard to understand why my soul passed
into this world a short while,
only to be taken so soon.
It seems cruel and unfair
from where you're standing
but try to look at it from mine…

I was born into a world that did not allow
for a gentle, sensitive spirit as mine.

Your earthly world is cold and harsh
it continually tries to break the spirit.
I tried my best to beat it,
to harden myself like other's
But my spirit was not made that way.
It was easily broken,
and after much battering and bruising,
it simply broke in two.
I could not put it back together again.
My soul yearned for the tranquillity and gentleness
it was born into.
My soul chose to give up the battle
and lead the way back home.

Do not think of me as gone,
as being worse off than you,
for although my body has returned to dust
my spirit remains with you.

Do not look for me like you used to,
for I will not be there.
Rather, look for me in the sun
that rises in the morning
and sets in the evening.
Look for me in the springtime flowers
and the autumn leaves.
Listen for me in the nightingale's song,
the wind in the trees
and the roar of the ocean.

Listen to all I have told you.
I have passed from this world
and returned to the other.
I am no longer broken.
I rest quietly,
in the warmth of the sun,
and sleep peacefully,
by the light of the moon.

Forgotten Garden

Walk with me
through a garden of graves

a forgotten garden
where nobody prays

avenues of souls
and anchors of love

witnessing angels
without faith from above

structures of class
still dominate the past

decrepit stones and broken bones
packed in the valley like quarry stones

where guardians of the underworld
patrol and protect

and vines of history
remind us to forget

wildflowers sway
in the whispering breeze

rain clouds gather

above wrinkled trees

gothic arches and filigree motifs
stained with smoke and tears of grief

infants who entered
with breathless defeat

and adults who tiptoed
a life of retreat

moss and decay
rust and dust

a forgotten garden
is nature's way

II

The loss of innocence is inevitable, but the death of innocence disturbs the natural order.

Eleven

I was 11
when he kept me after school
my English composition
a convenient excuse
I still remember the title
In the land of the dreadful buggaboos
He praised my creativity
admitted bemusement over the title
and finally asked me
to lean closer
pointing to the space
where his red ink
                        met my imaginative words
until I could feel his breath
on my ear
smell the masculinity of his cologne
As I waited
for his scholarly advice
I never expected
his hand to slip between my legs
and tell me that it was my fault.

Predators

Predators make lousy gardeners.
They pick buds from backyards
And strip flowers of their opportunity to bloom.

Obsession

His obsession builds
like a wild storm
on the horizon
and I watch — helplessly -
as it draws nearer
as the sound of thunder
- rattles -
and flashes of light
- strike -
filling me with dread
filling my insides
with liquid darkness
keeping my life
under perpetual nightfall.

Hunter

Mother offered him my teenage bed
- oblivious -
and he took it
couldn't wait to lie in it
breathing the scent
of a trophy
after years of fruitless tracking

The hunter, exhilarated
by the very thought
of closing in,
turns to his wife, the lowly substitute,
to enact the fantasy
that is destined for reality.

Hostage

She watches him
- from across the table -
mouth moving
licentious words
escalating
piercing her flesh
like fangs
splitting her ears
with his forked tongue
sinful eyes
burrowing
into pockets of innocence
relentlessly smashing the door
to her inner sanctum.
- Weakened -
by years of hostage
she counts the hands of despair
as her pink glow
pales
Her weaponry of words
fail
to deflect the vile flow
that inches closer.

His Sin

She suffers silently
Agonises so quietly
For his sin.

Her life tainted
Her innocence violated
For his sin.

Her past irrevocable
Her future inevitable
For his sin.

She stands alone
The choice not her own
For his sin.

Help

H-E-L-P
four simple letters
trapped in my throat

Help
a treacherous word
stitched behind my lips

Help
an impotent word
imprisoned by my silence

H-E-L-P
choke
bleed
expire.

III

Depression is a void of perpetual darkness. Left too long, the darkness is mistaken for light and the void a haven.

The Absence of Happiness

The absence of happiness, knowledge
withheld by teachers of misery, schooling
reserved for masters. Sadness
substitutes blood, veins
blue thoughts that hang, the precipice
cradles fragility.

Thoughts carry the weight of bones, psyche
trapped by a body of skeleton, joints
fixed into meandering associations feeding
rivers that swell and flood, oceans
forming like moats, vulnerable
and protected
inside an island castle.

Sadness

Sadness climbs inside me
settling itself uninvited
abducting wise discernment
exacerbating the splinters in my head
prompting a myriad of images
to roll
like a forbidden reel of film
causing emotional disquiet
propelling to the surface
ultimately untrammelled
emotional swells
take the shape of salty tears
welling, flowing, rolling down my cheeks
settling in moist droplets
all around me.
Sadness washes out of my entire being
cleansing
like a thundery rainstorm
until my catharsis is complete.

BLEED

In her mind
nothing makes sense
confusion is the passenger.

Myriad thoughts
colliding at top speed
for reasons she chose to abandon.

An abyss of slumber
forged by need
to forget the thoughts
that make her bleed.

Depression

Depression is a game,
my mind a player
Light leaks
from my wounded heart
Internal debris pollutes
my soul
Crimson handcuffs
secure my oppression
Help
is a mirage that wavers
on an imaginary horizon.

Darkness

Darkness eclipses light
like death on life.
Darkness occupies temperament
like anger on body.
Darkness occupies space
ineludible as a shadow.
The struggle for dominion
is soon to be won.
Darkness distorts light,
casts skyscraper shadows.
Darkness seeps into life
like groundwater.

Thought Tunnel

I slip inside the old thought tunnel
skin extinguished by darkness
falling prey to adolescent fears
struggling against the onslaught
of viscous gloom
that fills and floods
my body
breathing is for the bold
and the well-adjusted
the haves and the hordes
She invites me
into the cool echo
of dark familiarity
Attempts to coax me
into her throat
but she is wicked
She'll only let me drown
in her belly
and spit me out
Slipping inside the old thought tunnel
too scared to surrender
to the cool echo of dark familiarity.

The Mirror

She approaches its gilded frame
with apprehension and knotted insides
Peers into its shallow depths
Searching for the meaning of her
Contemplating with anxiety
the image reflecting back
Seeking physical acceptance
lacking within

Porcelain Ribs

Her porcelain ribs
steer her toward the frigid lake
where an insatiable monster
resurfaces in ripples
like a pebble
skimming glassy water

Wincing
at the distorted image
that swims and reflects
through merciless eyes
intent on ravaging
susceptible organs
with its inherent bitterness

On the brink of breathing
until the monster hauls her south
into the trembling mouth of the abyss
where crippling thoughts assemble
and grow in clumps of horned weeds

Aching for acceptance
but the monster's blood
courses her veins
swamping every space

The mirage of reprieve
dissipates

with the ripples in the lake
the monster retreating
into her porcelain ribs.

Unlovable

Sometimes
I want to empty myself
through my pen
until the ink runs dry
other times
I want to deface the words
that I have written
when there is not enough love reciprocated.
I am invaded
an interior frontier
of melancholy
I vacated myself
and forgot my smile behind.
My oxidized edges,
hazardous
at ease in the space
between solitude and silence.
Waiting to be abducted,
by misery that possesses me.
Searching for a key
that may not exist.
Saline fills my veins
instead of blood
holding out my hand
in moments of weak trust
pulling it back
when I feel the pinch
of paranoia

the reminder that nobody
truly loves me.
Cul-de-sac connections -
I will not let them in,
like I did the others, who
trampled the gardens of solitude
with their work boots.
Saline leaks from my soul
with overwhelming self-loathing
not even those who conceived me
were capable of loving me -
yet love lives in me
it constantly tries to escape
but it is tainted,
tainted, it must be
for it is always returned,
like an unopened envelope.
Perhaps it is postage
I know nothing about...
nothing to do with the love
I send
perhaps it's the receivers
who conceal a love impediment.
Love,
an acquaintance,
to be kept at arms length.
Whatever the reason
unopened love
buries my bones in a shallow grave
overshadows my soul

tears thoughts from my head,
like paper discarded
from the notepad - on which I confess -
Layers of skin,
pared
to the dispassionate skeleton
- that houses my restless spirit -
Just like me
my love
is not of this world
it doesn't belong now,
nor will it ever
belong
for I
am unlovable.

Rain

Standing in the rain
outside a locked gate
in vain

Standing in the rain
the darkness of the gorge
willing me

Standing in the rain
a phantom of a person
asking why?

Standing in the rain
with the same question
that plays its haunted melody
Why?
Why her, and not me?

IV

There are those whose love awakens our own and those whose love undermines.

Vulnerable

I am a book of pages
scribbled over with invisible ink
But he sees it all
like an international spy
or criminal mastermind

And I should feel vulnerable
while Rejection lingers
like a wisp of smoke
between us

But my secrets have become
weapons in themselves
and I am not afraid of dying

THE WIND

The wind blows so gently
And you breathe with gentle sighs
The soft movement
undisturbing to the trees
You lie asleep, breathing peacefully
a miracle of life
the mystery of wind
Breath gives life, breath gives wind
Miracle and mystery, breath and wind
Both so peaceful
Both have sinned.

In Reality

In my dream
you caress my face
- tenderly, lovingly -
In reality
you never do

In my dream
you take my hand in yours
- tenderly, reassuring -
In reality
you never do

In my dream
you embrace me
- openly, lovingly -
In reality
you never do

In my dream
you walk beside me
- proudly, respectfully -
In reality
you never do

In my dream
you hear me
- attentive, acknowledging -

In reality
you never do

In my dream
you call my name
- passionately, lovingly -
In reality
you never do

In my dream
you love me
- reciprocating, sincerely -
In reality
you don't.

If

If I could touch you
If my hands were free
Would my imagination abandon me?

If our bodies united
If our beings agreed
Would my heart be constant?

If the distance that lies between
Was swallowed into nothing
Would our souls be fixed?

If I had your sweetest word
If our barriers were broken
Would our lives be different now
or is this all unspoken?

WASTED

What if I've wasted precious time
Convincing my head your heart was mine
Wondering if we were meant to be
Have I been acting foolishly?

After giving all my hopes and dreams
Never concealing my whims or needs
You've taken all with little thought
These special things that can't be bought.

If God had only given me
The things I've handed you for free
A special gift to cherish and keep
Never meaning for me to weep.

Will I be given back the key
To heal my heart and set you free?

Loved and Lost

I have tried so hard
I have given so much
bared my soul
and exposed my heart

You have manipulated
You have been devilishly cruel
and calculated

I have loved and lost
You have merely lost.

Unrequited Love List

I loved you with every breath
my bones ached for you
my heart beat faster for you
my stomach flipped and fluttered for you
you pried the secrets that I hid from the world
you painstakingly won my trust only to betray it
you offered me your hand only to kick me back down
we lived during the night
I looked past your lies,
your manipulations,
your humiliations,
your mindful torture,
your withholding emotions,
your disrespect,
your volatility,
your cruelty,
you nurtured my self-loathing until
I beat myself up worse than you ever could
passionate love and post-coital loathing
you used my vulnerability as a weapon against me
you pretended to care and then left me all alone
put me out in the cold
questioning myself,
your words like poisoned arrows
your violence splintered inside my bones
your name burrowed into my skin
your misogyny moulded my body
your name became a permanent tattoo

you were the eclipse that never ended
my shadow withered in your darkness
your imprint as indelible as blood spatter.

LOVE STORM

My heart rate trebles
when he walks in
Certain the whole room can hear it
sing

He weakens every limb
sets every nerve a tingling
overloads all six senses
renders my soul naked

I cannot explain
this gravitational pull
I cannot explain

When he looks at me
I melt,
- exposed, vulnerable, irrational -
hopeless free-fall
what am I to do?

I am repeatedly struck down
by the lightning
of our wild love storm

We delude the present
dance around the past
tease about the future

He tells me that he loved me,
but I broke his heart -
I tell him, it was the other way around.

Merlot Heart

My merlot heart. Seduced.
By mythic tales of thousand year old sun-worshippers.
Gazed directly into that fiery star
- too long -
Traded moon boots for gravity
And now
the surface gloss of decades,
belies the grain
of light years below.

My merlot heart,
once pulsing to a haunting melody,
now labours to a tired tune.
Unable to recreate the elation of that moonwalk.
Euphoria. Inaccessible,
beyond the space between dreams
and that black hole
of indelible memory.

My merlot heart,
bleeding its colour
in a disappearing world,
where the sun is but a star,
and the moon, a whole planet.

Desire

Desire dawned on a vermilion summer night
His feathered charm faded into the salmon canvas
with the waning light of day
His flaming desire spilled into my pink passion
for the last time

I desired her more
Her feminine grace
I desired more of our rose-scented days
her fluid sensuality clinging like gold leaf
to my naked skin
flowers gleamed gold in her nurturing shadow

She was summer
in my winter room
Electric storms
and earth tremors, she ignited
inside my arid body

As my hunger for him dwindled
His winged charm toiled to entice
his beak curled in anticipation
but his love elixir no longer
satiated my hearts thirst
frustration flattened his titillated crest
his ego strutted about helplessly
the natural order confused

Desire dawned on a vermilion summer night
he loved me like a jewel
she, breath itself
he burned me with his lust
and his feathered charm faded with the waning light of day
I found refuge in her floral-scented skin
Pink passion spilled onto the salmon canvas
and I basked in the twilight of her desire.

V

If dreams are the wings of your soul, a cage will surely kill them.

Purpose

What is my purpose?
I repeat to self
Is it in vain?
uncertainty only knows

Am I holding on?
hoping against the odds,
that doggedly disrupts my progress,
that life will transmute

Will fate intervene?
taking destiny with it
Or is it my intervention
that destiny waits upon?

Do I know the answers
to rhetorical questions?
How potent is my power
to dive inside
and swim inside my truth?

Death Star

A galaxy dwells inside us
stars of prospects and possibilities beckon
unimaginable adventure awaits
yet lulled by the security of gravity
immobilised by the death star.

Borderless horizons beckon our intent
but the death star looms in our imagined universe
exploration limits are not decided,
they levitate at our beck and call
the death star reigns without sovereignty.

Gravity keeps us earth-bound
while our destiny floats in space
resistance fuels the death star's power
where meteor showers are commonplace
and shooting stars are improbable as unicorns.

Faceless

Trapped inside
a corporate cage
suspended
in a shallow sky.

Restrictive chains
for a daily wage
while your soul
slowly
dies.

Tangled
in the corporate vine
searching the faceless
for a familiar sign.

Sky

Focus, suspended in a marbled sky
pastel blue significance filters in patches
through an opaque cloud of worlds
Casting bait-laden lines into turquoise streaks
where schools of silver-winged flying fish
journey toward that mythical ocean in the sky.

The mouth of the sky laughs, revealing mountains
beyond its throat
and I search for its limbs, toes, fingers - anything to use as a ladder
to climb - but all I see is that mouth
My only way up is to fly, but my earthly wings lie in tatters
I reach out and ask,
but my voice is carried west
by passing winds
weakened by the noise of the world
I tell myself, if I can see that mountain in the sky
then there must be a way to reach it
before long, the laughing is only in my head
the sky mouth, closed
the marbled sky my reality.

Dreams

The future,
fearful
at times
of what it holds.

Such vivid dreams.
In reality,
seem so bold.

Plunge
into the dream lake
one day at a time.
Transform your reality
into a life
sublime.

Success

The sky constantly gathers up clouds in her arms
Will I ever chase down that cloud called 'Success'?
It seems a professional shape-shifter...

So many times, it has pulled its tongue at me
Unleashed apocalyptic rain
onto the road I travel
Washed me into gutters,
filled with failures debris.

At times I stop running,
stop chasing,
slow down,
adjust my view to horizontal

I watch that cloud from beneath
watch it float past sunshine
and disappear
into the milky way.

Yesterday

I cast my thoughts back to yesterday's river
when youth was an altered concept
and passionate pursuits were mine,
in those troubled waters
where I uprooted every weed of injustice,
regardless of opposition

Age has not caught up to me -
I realise -
Yet, youth's buoyancy has long been adrift

But, when I glimpse my reflection in the river of today -
even with the sage of experience washing over me
and the trees of good intention bending and dipping their
heads into the compliant waters of tranquillity -
the jagged edges of rocks, once carved by youth's enslavement,
are submerged beneath the rising waters of maturity
and I,
have forgotten myself
in yesterday.

VI

Those who nurse secrets, nurse a chaotic world of amplified silence.

Death Addiction

When the door to suicide opens, it becomes a viable option that you never considered before. Once ajar, it initiates an invasion strategy; day by day, thoughts blacken under the occupation of the new inhabitant until it becomes an all-consuming addiction that makes its home in your head and heart. Before you know it, the whole neighbourhood is talking and thinking about suicide. Eventually, the mind is overwhelmed by the conspiracy of its own darkness and begins to wage war against the body. At this point, the body is powerless.

Amplified Silence

Violence interrupted, disrupted
vandalised the skeleton of skin

Innocence abducted
without anaesthetic

Reborn in the perpetrators shadow
a synthetic mutation that victimised itself

Decanted bottomless despair
swallowed promises of ecstasy

Chased the light of a soul down dark alleys
before it vanished in the blinking strobe

Hijacked by depression
Suicide in the passenger seat

Drove to the valley of graves
to dig 6 feet of repression

Buried the secret alive
each shovel of dirt amplified the silence

Perforated

The final alarm sounded
in grey passageways
after a morning with G.
Into the passenger seat, I shrunk
artificial sentiment
competed for oxygen
inside her white knight.
I dwelled on passing omens –
a convoy of black hearses
a yard of graves -
before we slipped
from the N3 mouth
into the bowels of Little India.

Her white knight bleached
the littered streets.
Her sweaty hand steered me,
like a rudder though the Ganges,

through a parallel world of vibrance –
red chillies and orange curry powder,
yellow turmeric and sticks of cinnamon,
green dunya, still smelling of earth and rain –

a parallel world of difference –
of hustle and haggle
hypnotic rhythm and Bollywood beats
worship echoing from Grey Street Mosque

colourful shrines to Ganesh -
Reminders of M – yet another woman, oppressed.

We cut through textiles,
eyes hemmed between fabric
-turquoise, fuchsia, sunflower and gold -
'til we reach my fate.

My chaperone ushers me inside
a room, as lightless as my life,
with furniture, as threadbare as my soul,
opposite a doctor without an oath.

He shoves two strips
of purple jewels
into my hand
and holds up an index finger
as instruction.

My fingers clasp
his untreated gift
Eyes fixated
on the rows of relief,
designed to feed
my insatiable demons...

Hours later,
alone again,
Hostile thoughts
hijack my body.

I take one purple jewel after the next
and watch the perforated strips
fall
to the polished floor.

Eclipse

Horizontal, on a bed
arms and legs, splayed
head hanging -
half on, half off -
Eyes rolling back,
intermittently
Skin pulled tight
over tear-stained bones
- Eclipse -
Sobs subside as pills hit
an unlined stomach
Horizontal, vulnerable, alone.
Her mind's sky, cluttered
with cloud cover
body and mind, segregated
her heavy head, weighs her down, with thoughts of personal
terrorism
attempts to extricate her from decades of desperation
Her dilated pupils, search
for the source of
voices, and strange chatter -
futile –
all she finds is hands -
poking through the glass panel above the door;
regular hands that stretch into arms, spread along the walls
that enclose her
Horizontal, mesmerised, curious –
Her heavy lids blink and close like lens-shutters.

4 Days Later

she wakes inside an empty flat
alone, confused
memories, unobtainable
flashbacks, penetrate like spies

not a soul in sight
reminded of the abandonment
reminded of the lonely existence that stretches ahead
the financial flood for which there is no lifeboat

she glimpses her pale, thin reflection
traces of black stain her mouth
she picks up the phone
and dials the pharmacy.

Insomnia

I watch his moped sail past
from my window over the Berea
his smile as fresh as the
rainbow souvenir flag at his back
flapping like a ribbon in the hot, January air.

I wait for the buzzer to sound
trembling finger poised to release
the gate to my prison
listen for the echo of his footsteps
up two flights of stairs.

I stitch up my desolate loneliness
with a superficial smile
wipe the trace of black liquid
that stains my lips
to greet him with my insomnia.

This will help you sleep
he offers kindly
then turns to leave
on my nod and smile

Little does he know
that my insomnia is world-related
and nothing to do with sleep.

The Other Side

Horizontal again
between the weight of two bodies
from the other side
A dark, hooded shadow awakens fearful curiosity
A woman's glittery outline reminds her of love
Another hallucination?
His icy fingers freeze her fleeting smile
and stop her questions in their tracks
His icy fingers close around her neck
permanent abduction
Hot, mortal danger surges like electricity
rushes from tip to top
Victory is his if she doesn't fight
Survival floods her body
giving her just enough strength
to claw and scratch her way
out of his icy grip
and into the warmth
of the glitter queen.

Answers

I force myself
through the doors of resurrection
head hung in shame
for my unforgivable choice
On bended knee,
I thank you
- for rejecting me -
I strain to hear you whisper,
from your cross of torment
an answer to my afflictions
I search your book for directions
that will sweep me away
from the perilous edge
where I sway like a drunk
I beg you to slow the winds
that could sweep me off my feet
at any given time

I lift my head in defiance
and beg your explanation
for the powerless years of torment
I implore you to alleviate the nightmares
that refuse to relent
to play me a melody
that does not haunt
to clear the chaos
of thoughts
that clutter and cloud

to set fire to my impediments
and let them burn to cinders

I ask with sincerity
why did both my fathers desert me?

LIFE

"Sometimes you have to cross the boundaries of Death in order to discover the meaning of Life."

Death and Life II

Life
forgets death.
Infants breathe in, youth springs forth,
healthy bodies burgeoning
love echoes life, hearts dance together
friends and lovers, marriage of families
time melts away, age creeps in
Dreams of slumber, darkness squeezing light
Death waits patiently
flesh and bones, dust to dust
age breathes out Life and Death
~ interrupting ~
Death and Life
Out breathes age
Dust to dust, bones and flesh
Patiently waits death
Light squeezing darkness, Slumber of dreams
In creeps age, away melts time
families of marriage, lovers and friends
together dance hearts, life echoes love
burgeoning bodies healthy
Forth springs youth, in breathe infants
Death forgets
Life.

VII

When you forsake your motherland, you cannot comprehend the fact that you will forfeit precious fragments of yourself in the process.

Forfeit

I must forfeit my life
uproot my poisoned feet
abandon my motherland.

I must forfeit my possessions,
but I am sentimental.
I'm afraid my memories will bleed
with the loss of each page
that fills the books of my youthful hope;
a lifeline of words
that suspended my sadness.

Each and every one of those books
more brilliant than diamonds -
No
I will forfeit clothes for books
for I cannot forfeit Emily's words,
where I wandered those barren moors
breathlessly intoxicated by Heathcliff's raw emotion.

And what of the paintings?
Unearthed in my birthplace
amidst Sunday flea markets
paintings that hung like muses
on my art deco walls.
And what of my first Klimt?
So utterly beloved.

What of these?
How am I to forfeit these things

that quicken my heart
and feed my soul?

I must forfeit my madness
by destroying my journals
lest they use my words against me...
My truth is too cluttered
for their minimalist world
My words too heavy to roll off their tongues
My thoughts too bellicose to entertain.

I must forfeit all of these things
for the actions that will forever
hang in my skeleton closet
the only price,
my soul.

Survival

Survival depends on
- denial -
Denial of the hatred,
the violence,
the pain, the cruelty.
Denial of the ugliness
that moves like the wind
through streets,
cities, suburbs, townships.
Denial is all you have,
when you are on the ground
when ugliness is ubiquitous
violence
- inescapable -
Denial permeates your skin
bleeds into your veins
breaks your heart
aches in your bones
crashes inside your head.
Survival
- depends on denial -
and death comes swiftly
to those who forsake it.

Africa

Africa
My stomach knots
My head rages
thoughts stray and scatter
Like leaves lifting in a passing breeze

Africa
My heart palpitates
Somewhere
subconsciously
I am enchanted

Africa
My skin tingles
Radiant Sunshine
Wrapped in her warmth
alive again

Africa
my cradle – my grave
Ambiguity – conflict

Internal battlefield
Each time – Africa.

MOTHERLAND

I spent a lifetime in union with her
built strong foundations and anchored my roots
I wept tears of anguish for yesterday's sins
but smiled with hope for tomorrow's forgiveness.

I felt a traitor having left her
The one who holds the roots of my history
The one who keeps the secrets of the past
The one who has shaped my life thus far.

I am indebted to her always and forever
for nurturing my young life
for building my strength of character
for revealing the light and dark.

I have forsaken her for a place
I will never belong
But will always remain under her spell
Forever to be a child of my motherland.

Leaving

Silence swam between us
My thoughts suspended
precariously above me
Like a bank of top-heavy rain clouds
She knew nothing about leaving
But I knew
my thoughts persisting
swelling in silence
increasing in potency
Threatening to burst
If I moved a muscle
Or dared open my mouth
She had only been taken places
She was a swimmer
Wading into the cobalt ocean
On a clear day
Sheltered by azure skies and dazzling sunbeams
between red and yellow flags
Safe
under the watchful eyes of bronzed lifeguards
Rippling muscles at the ready
lest a stray current threatened
To strike
She didn't know that vital parts of you stayed behind
Essential parts, cherished parts
Planted and anchored in the old place
Dense roots, resolute and mulish
no matter how violently you tried to dislodge them

in order to take them with you
Like a sea of glass
Aquamarine water, calm on the surface
but underneath
there are burly currents
and noxious weeds
threatening to engulf you
dragging you under
and drowning you mutely
beneath the surface.

EXTRADITION

I traverse virtual streets
of my skeleton past;
hear the echo of ghosts and ghouls
that no longer walk those crumbling streets,
but turn in buried coffins
that exist in the graveyard of my mind
and cobwebs of a shrouded memory -
their decaying bones and misty remains
a reminder
of life before extradition.

Layers of complexity, pared
with the skill of a surgeon
scrutinised by the eye of a magnified glass
only to reveal the truth of what was denied
and yet
my insides still ache from the weight of my first life
where I drowned in my own indifference.

I force the act of forgetting
for I know I cannot return
to that parallel world
that cradles my youth
and entombs my failed beginnings.
A broken world
from which I miraculously exited
and which I now visit and view
with the pleasure and horror

of an impassive voyeur.

I long to belong,
but accept that I am incompatible
with fear and hate and anger and violence.
I want a medal for my time in extradition
but I am undeserving;
I chose this battle and I am no veteran,
nor am I one of the ghostly ghouls
that walk that bloodstained land
of unrivalled beauty and unimaginable brutality.
I yearn to release my fettered grip
of that mystical motherland
that loved and hated,
healed and broke,
kissed and spat
accepted and rejected
her own child.

I am born in Africa,
but I live
 in extradition.

Migrant Skin

I am a migrant
collecting years like postage stamps
a countdown to belonging...

My migrant skin remembers
its motherland
My roots
haunt me at night
My memories suspended
like morning fog across the intersections of my life
then and now.

My migrant skin
is visible
when I speak
My inflection labels me
as foreign
an expat of my tainted motherland
Forever guilty by association
I am.
My migrant skin longs to belong
but cannot deny the knowledge
that it is destined to be
pre-judged and neatly packaged
into migrant moulds that cannot be broken
by desire, or time.

My migrant skin does not belong

here nor there
It is a hybrid:
shining in the gloss of photos
sent to those left behind
A misshapen jigsaw piece
superfluous to the new puzzle.

I don't know how to tell you,
that we chose each other,
that my collection is 7 years strong,
yet my migrant skin blushes
with the pretence of a foreigner.

I'm talking to you.
I'm asking you to look at me,
to listen to me;
I am a migrant
who wants to contribute
with diversity to offer,
compassion to lend,
with stories to tell.

I chose you over my motherland
and my story
is your story now.

VIII

I walked to an isolated beach, day after day, seeking companionship in the roar of the ocean, and contemplating the shipwreck of my life. There, in that isolated wilderness, amidst the screaming gulls, and consistent rhythm of the tides, I channelled my chaotic thoughts through my pen and released them into poetry, until the quiet desperation passed and I was secure in the knowledge that I had made it through another day.

Winter Landscape

How did I end up here?
So far away from my home
So far away from myself
An outcast in every sense
but,
in this void
of distant abandon
I caught sight of something
long forgotten
I heard the familiar sound
I felt the gentle touch
I saw the beautiful face
of my soul
beckoning me home
reminding me
that all was not lost
but instead, found
The tumultuous journey
misunderstood
for so long
now revealed in clarity.

Shipwreck

Violent waves subside.
The wind turns in exile.
Windswept hair exhales.
A murmur-less ocean kneels
and bows its head -
revealing the shipwreck
left behind.

Submerged below the cool surface,
reaching out to me.
A veneer of peace, from my secluded beach,
but the screaming gulls tell the truth...

I look down at my barnacled feet
and trails of blue bottles littering the path behind me;
the transparency of stranded jellyfish.

Drowned ships cannot be floated.
Shipwrecks belong underwater;
the best they can offer is exploration.

Seek

The things I seek
are carried by the wind .
During intervals of emotional stillness
and inner silence
I seek it out .
Searching for the source ;
Traces - of where I am meant to go -
to find solace - about where I have been.
As the waves sweep the ocean bed
so my past sweeps my soul
carrying with it
remnants - of yesterday's sorrow -
and sweeps forth
fragments - of a brighter tomorrow.

Journey

I journey
barefoot
along Mairangi sand
a pen and notebook -
my only companion, my saving grace -

I meditate
beside waveless waters
of the Pacific
soothe scattered thoughts -
that rasp in my head –

I listen
to uninhibited screams
of red-billed gulls -
they voice their freedom to the skies –

I write
filling blank pages
like blood fills veins -
captive words echoing in silence –

I journey barefoot
pen poised
beside waveless waters
Listening
to voices of freedom
filling blank pages

with bloody words
that echo in captivity.

THE PATH

Reflective glass
invites my glance
into a writer's window,
where a sunken seat
houses the modern typewriter.

Book-lined walls,
Heavy with knowledge.
Climbing ivy,
Reaching the height of Jack's beanstalk.

Red flowering Pohutukawa's
lead me down the path.
Bark swathed in green moss.
Seaward-reaching branches,
strain
to hear whispering waves
of Mairangi Beach.

The Ocean Heaves

The ocean heaves
with laboured movements
Straining
to push
the grey expanse
toward the rocky shoreline
Exhaling,
as she unleashes a swell,
Sighing
She lingers,
Until a bellow reverberates.
Inhaling sea mist,
Her energy restored,
She begins again.

TO THE ROCKS

I shimmy
around the decrepit trunk -
Touch the cicatrices
of grey and white grooves.

Leviathan waves
break
over sea lion boulders -
Whiskers submerged,
momentarily,
until the tide swirls
away
like bathwater down a plughole.

I have made it
To the rocks.

The Secret Bench

Salted sea air
is undependable,
so today,
my senses flirt
with the elusive scent
that capers and sibilates
off curling waves.

Pinned by the bend,
I clamber
up the tiara-stone-wall,
and find a secret bench -
nestled
amongst native bush,
sheltered
from the swaying breeze.

Seagull Party

Steely blue water
glistens
in the morning sun
Playing host to a party
of red-billed seagulls
- parading along sandbanks -
some bathe in rivulets
that run into the pacific,
while others bob,
lackadaisical,
on the water -
model-sized yachts
in America's Cup.

A red-billed gull
erupts
into a shrill cry,
beak wide open
head rolled back
into the downy nook of its neck…

The sun takes no notice,
lounging in the sky
on the long white cloud.

The Night Moves

Absinthe bay
cradles Devonport
Evening folds,
gaining heaviness
Islands juxtaposed
kelp layers marooned,
nutmeg and orange -
Naked overnight.
Palpate queen
rises
from Rangitoto,
serenading Takapuna
until velvet water
exhales
its youthful zeal.

SELF-DISCOVERY

Since I've been away,
from family and friends,
I have found myself.
A wondrous sensation
of excitement,
and internal stability -
Fortuitous equanimity.

Slowly unearthing,
who I am,
what I am,
what my needs are, my beliefs
what my fears are, and hopes -
Focus and direction
no longer amorphous
but gradually, crystallising.

Elucidating self:
my views breathe with dignity,
my feelings, an ocean to explore,
my freedom, no longer captive,
emancipated through the journey
of self-discovery.

SEARCHING

I have been searching
the great sky above
the expansive waters below
what have I found?

I have been searching
dirty nightclub holes
faces, of people I know
What have I found?

I have gone within
the depths of my core
what I have found
I need search no more.

IX

We had lunch everyday in an historic church yard, to the delight of hungry sparrows, talking with ease and sharing an unspoken understanding. At first, I didn't think it was love, for I only knew the perilous love of yesterday, whereas this, this felt safe.

Protector of my heart

Fragments
of your tender voice
soothe
my noisy thoughts
your love
has come to rescue me

I have finally found you
protector
of my heart
Before me, you stand
with the love of a caretaker
hand outstretched,
offering, a gilded key
to unlock
my shackled heart.

The Kiss

I close my eyes
seeking refuge from my surroundings
enveloped
in his arms
sheltered
by a blanket of protection
I drift beyond the harshness
and leave it all behind

He releases me
for a moment
looking down at me
searching for comfort in my eyes
We are mesmerised
caught up
in the silent security
of one another

My eyes close
when the kiss befalls me
Like silk on skin
and sun on my face
Enraptured
by the sweet sensation
Swept away
on the waves of eternity

He embraces me

once again

and I retreat
to the sanctuary of his arms.

Dance Me To The End Of Love

Our love is a dance in progress
Set under the spotlight of inexperience
The day we joined hands in union
We took up our positions
As partners in the dance
Two hearts set in rhythm, the music plays.

Together we stand tall, heads held high
Facing the music, regardless of the beat
Never too close to stifle
Nor too far to fall out of sync
Striving gracefully, toward a common goal.

Each year our dance advances
Embracing each new step, as a lesson to learn
A challenge to meet
Always considerate, of each other's dreams
as we move together on the dance floor of life.

As the lights begin to dim, and the music quietens
We look to our silhouettes,
as a glimpse into the past
Appreciating memories, that lie imprinted
on the backdrop of a life in fullness
Saying to each other,
Dance me, to the end of love.

Love Garden

Spring flowers burst first with sunny thirst
We nursed our garden, love sprouting,
never doubting through seasonal pouting.
Through summer heights and sultry nights
immune to fights, two hearts merged
and our lives converged.

Our hearts sang when Winter sprang,
marriage bells rang, we were ying and yang.
Honey and moons and late afternoons
coffee and teaspoons, red conversations
and blue revelations in our garden of patience.
No cloud too black to knock us off track.

But neglected weeds strangle needs
and discontent breeds
stunting relationship seeds.
Temptation creeps and doubt seeps
conclusion leaps.
From our lips, sprout spiky quips
coldness grips and tolerance is lost in our garden of frost.

Love kept us brave, lovers forgave,
and we found a way to save our garden from grave.
Through countless seasons, we overcame reasons
for underlying treasons.
With honest words shared, two lovers repaired
a love once snared.

Our garden blooms and love echoes in our wombs.

Liebe

The Vienna secession framed our epic love
Two hearts budding into Spring's first rose
Hands joined by gold circles of eternity
Dimming the silhouettes of youth's ghosts
Lovers forged in flames of passion
A Liebe worthy of Shakespeare's sonnets

Our union, Petrarch's muse, praised in sonnets
Klimt's canvas a testament to our love
Pens poised to chronicle the heights of our wild passion
Annals of liebe dedicated to love's blossoming rose Artists
hands painting vilified faces of bygone ghosts
Songs written to the tune of eternity

A garden of Eden that flourishes for eternity
buds that blossom into flowering sonnets
Summer breezes sweep away whispers of scorned ghosts
row upon row, grow seeds of love
lover's wings alighting like a butterfly from a rose
only a honey bee in search of pollen would fathom our passion

Every breath, every dream, every heartbeat born of passion
a fever that will burn from now until eternity
the Sun's fiercest rays powerless to wilt our rose
a desire that possesses the muse and fuels sonnets
an earthly union that ascends to the heavens of love
impervious to the vengeful glower of loves erstwhile ghosts

Ghoulish faces of lovers scorned, linger in the background like ghosts
incapable of quelling their singular passion
unwilling pawns in the game of unrequited love
trapped betwixt the world of love and hate 'til eternity
wailing like lovers scorned, in maudlin sonnets
withering like sun-faded petals of a neglected rose

Stems of history strengthen our beauteous rose
her thorns of green protect against lingering ghosts
A rose to wax lyrical about in celebrated love sonnets
The laughter of offspring sustaining our passion
A union that endures the trials of mortality, for an eternity
From Spring's first bud to the burgeoning rose that is our love

A rose for all seasons, our sacrosanct Love
Chasing ghosts of lovers past into the clouds of Eternity
Filling books of sonnets with our amaranthine Passion

X

Secrets have the power to imprison. Confessions have the power to liberate.

Dream Cocoon

The light tower blinks and wanes.
Waves of sleep,
crash at her aching feet.
Wild wind rushes
around her smooth curves.

Calls her,
Nudges her,
Teases her,
Wills her,
to freedom.

She succumbs;
her body exhales life.
She escapes;
her soul inhales freedom.

A dream passenger;
journeying
on invisible wings, rushing
through clouds of yesterday
- where she left her smile -
Soaring above ravines
of faces and fears
that once held her captive.
Dancing
in fields of the future
to refuel her waking dreams.

The hollow sound
Of waves crashing
reverberates
inside her dream cocoon.

Calls her,
Nudges her,
Teases her,
Wills her
back
to her light tower,
that bathes beneath
the copper sky.

Mara

After years of searching
and much trepidation
I was prepared to find her .
To meet her
With my bruises, battle wounds, and scars .
I was going to see her
speak to her.
My stomach pounding,
alive with the flutter of a thousand butterflies .
Here I was, in Hampstead Heath
In a strange room,
with a strange woman
But , f e e l i n g
Feeling strangely soothed .
Her wild black hair,
and penetrating chocolate eyes
Boring into the dark places
of my heart, and head, and soul.
I began talking,
anxiously at first,
but then I picked up a rhythm
And all the monstrous things,
the deep grievances,
the cruel experiences
came rushing at me
in a flood
Bombarding me
in such a way

that the words began to
r o l l
off my tongue
Uncontrolled,
without restraint.
I talked, and talked, and talked .
E m p o w e r e d
Until I was empty .
All the wretchedness
- drained away -
blood stains – cleansed -
The confusion, dread, fear,
and quiet awfulness
that once lay festering,
lurking
was unshackled .
Flooding
and overflowing
bringing with it,
L i b e r a t i o n
A feeling
that had only lived in dreams
but now,
found its way into reality .
This strange woman,
M a r a
an intimate friend
I had never known
An earth mother, life giver,
freer of my chains.

Jar of Secrets

I carried my jar of secrets
step by childhood step
through prickly clumps of wild grass
and filmy spider nets.

I dug my nails into my hand
step by blistered step
as I crossed the solar powered tar
and dunes of scorching sand.

I placed my jar of glass and tin
at her capricious feet
I offered her my broken body
and whispered my defeat.

I floated in her cool embrace
watched the ebony drift away
in her weightless world of love
I saw another way.

She ebbed and flowed toward my jar
of glass and secret sin
and released it back into the blue
from whence it did begin.

Proposal

When I peer into life's mirror
the cicatrices of healing is unmistakable
so too, is a fading personality and spirit -
like a vibrant print
subjected to sun exposure,
too long -

New Zealand's solitude
and isolated shores
has served my rehabilitation.
My whispering heart
proposes
a new path.

My hand-stitched wings itch
to take flight.
To test the winds of change
that inevitably blow
at the end
of a cycle.

Goodbye Rangi

Cerise transports me along the bays
Past Milford marina
Who lies lethargic
As a glass lake.

Passing through Mairangi
Long-lashed sea mist
Blinks, seductively
Teasing in swells.

Climbing up the hill to Rothesay
Past the blue gold Thai
Where my love proposed
with diamonds and nerves
And the old lady
provides refuge to wild birds.

XI

When I liberated myself from religion, and its patriarchal propaganda, I was no longer the forgotten female - fated to an eternity of subservience - but a defiant female who acknowledged that the dictatorship would last as long as I allowed it.

When I discarded the idea, or parked alongside the realisation, that God was not necessarily a man (as I had been raised to think and believe without question) I grew distant.

As I accelerated away from what I knew, that ungovernable distance grew, and the flame that once lit my path began to flicker and hiss like a candle burnt to its wick, making longevity impossible without a new energy source.

As I detoured past each patriarchal disruption and religious contradiction, the source of my self-loathing became evident and a pattern of feminine deaths emerged. As I journeyed through intersections of unlearning and relearning the dogmatic flavours of my life soured until unpalatable and I became increasingly alienated from the 'God' that had once been second nature.

That alienation and disconnection peaked during times of prayer. In childhood, my maternal grandmother had fostered the habit of bedtime prayer - a habit that had instilled a sense of comfort and hope - and the unquestioned belief that God would, overnight, protect every animal, child, woman, and man while I slept. Of course, with age, realisation dawned that God did not take care of the world overnight, or anytime for that matter.

Unquestioned belief gave rise to a highway of unanswered questions and inconsistencies that I was incapable of reconciling. This God and his religion had been used to colonise people, tribes and ancient traditions. This God had been instrumental in the ideology of segregation and Apartheid. This God had dictated sexuality and condemned difference.

This God gifted free will, but took away responsibility. This God fostered a false sense of security and contradicted my natural instincts by aligning them with guilt and shame. This God condemned suicide, and I couldn't understand how personal pain and suffering was a basis for judgment instead of forgiveness. The more I thought about it, the less sense this God made.

    The complete disconnect finally came when I separated the concepts Man-God, then God-Church. It was clear from my destructive experiences with feminine persecution that patriarchy was neatly aligned with my 'old God', and this knowledge gave rise to an inevitable death. Except, it was a death without mourning – for my grief had already taken place, year after year, under the paradigm of patriarchal religion and a God who was well versed in the hypocrisy of love, but who in fact was nothing more than vengeful, judgemental and sexist. Furthermore, when I separated the concepts God and church, all I was left with was religion, which, as it turned out, was just another form of control, a powerful form of government, patriarchal heaven. I finally asked myself the nagging question that had been graffitied on every single road sign of my life - if the 'old God' was a man, who never lived up to his reputation, then what exactly was I hanging onto, and why? Moreover, if I was to liberate myself from that regime and its propaganda, then what did my future look like? In truth, it meant obliterating the status quo of my former paradigm. It meant the death of God and the meaning of my authentic life.

    Judgement day finally arrived for God and the league of dogmatic patriarchs, who had oppressed the first 23 years of my life, during my enlightening journey toward life. Once

I absorbed the truth that the God from my childhood was a patriarchal God, and I, as the forgotten female, was fated to an eternity of subservience (if I stayed the old course), I accepted that the dictatorship would last as long as I allowed it. I, as an intelligent and defiant female, did not belong to that subservient line; my knowledge and courage empowered me to end female oppression, both for myself and those girls and women who came after me. No more would I dilute my feminine power, no more would I accept their teachings, no more would I allow the double standards, no more would I view myself through their disparaging eyes, no more would I accept second best. No more.

The God from my childhood was officially dead, and the paradigm under which I had wilted and nearly died was disassembled, and carried away, piece by piece. I was no longer the female that God forgot, and blind submission was no longer my religion. I decided that if there was a superior being, then it was incapable of being labelled; it was fluid - without gender, race, sexuality, in fact, any societal constructs. Furthermore, if there was a superior being, then some part of it was living and breathing through me, and I, as an intelligent, compassionate, thinking, evolving soul, equipped with natural instincts, was more than capable of gaining wisdom through my own personal experience and not at all bound by the dictatorial rules and nonsensical regulations and judgements of a man-made paradigm. Furthermore, I was certain that the gift of free will was bestowed for a reason, and I recognised it as a huge responsibility. Free will held me, and nobody else, responsible and accountable for my own actions.

I do not reject the idea of a superior being, or miracles, or I have experienced all of those unquantifiable things. Instead, I choose to substitute man-made religion with spirituality. The way I see it, I give the superior being much more respect and gratitude by tapping into the potential that I've been born with, as opposed to judging myself as an inferior sinner who is nothing without the validation of a man-made paradigm.

Freedom

Freedom exists
in a fifth season
in a sixth sense
but they are walking wounded
their vision - impaired -
They anathematise my freedom
but they are prisoners in the end
for who would reject
another season,
another sense?

Monarch

Standing inside corners
cocooned by a wooden frame
A monarch butterfly floats by.

On a zephyr, she lingers
Willing me down spiral stairs
into the emerald garden
where sunshine peeks
from long white clouds.

Her freedom implores me
to tug at the silk
of my cocoon.

Her transformation, a reminder
that my bandages of silk were essential,
not wasted.

Her purpose reminds me
of my second chance
in this fleeting life.

Her presence, a reminder,
that I'm not alone.

The gold threads
in her powdery black wings
a reminder, of the sacred feminine

of intuition, of healing, of compassion.

Her courage in an uncertain world
encourages me to escape from my corners.
To acknowledge and release my gifts.
To test my wings, trust the breeze, and take flight.

A journey of meaning awaits,
but time
does not.

XII

*Change blows through the branches of our existence
and fortifies the roots on which we stand.*

Tree of Life

Change fortifies the roots on which we stand.
Change blows through the branches of our existence.
Change infuses crimson experience with autumn hues.
Change dismantles Winter's brittle leaves.
Change ushers Spring into our fertile environments,
where the seeds of evolution burst from their pod cocoons,
and teardrop buds blossom into Summer flowers.
Change releases its redolent scent;
attracting the buzz of honey bees
and the adoration of discerning butterflies.
Change breathes new life
into the Tree of Life.

Purple Hibiscus

Purple hibiscus
a hybrid of sorts
Usually startling red
but now,
punctured
red bleeding out,
blue pumping in

Purple hibiscus
Resistant at first
slowly succumbing
Realising,
Adaptation was not violation,
but evolution

Purple hibiscus
No longer wincing
at the blood-stained past
Aware
of the purple freedom
lying within.

Anchors

These material anchors
that tether us
to barnacled moorings
in shallow waters, where life is unlived.

The decommissioned lighthouse
a vestige of the dream, that the sky forgot
nothing more than a tourist attraction
with sunrise at its back.

Time trickles away
each time the tide turns its crested head
dragging wasted potential and missed opportunities
toward the tenebrous sunset.

These material anchors
that enslave before sunrise
hemming us into overcrowded harbours
their promise fading
into a mirage on the horizon
at dusk.

Liberty is a cold current;
acclimatised, we are not
The ocean is neither friend nor foe
and weather reports, unreliable.
Anchors are not immortal;
trail blazers have survived, untethered.

The ocean whispers
and sometimes roars
Summoning bold abandon.
So why not sail, toward horizons of change
to meet the waves of adventure
with the wind rising up to meet your courage
sweeping you along shores of discovery
and islands of escape?
Clouds disappearing behind
the sun's yawning smile.

Slumbering Queen

One thief
Leaves the moon on a trade wind
Landing feet first
upturned lavender bells
tinkling
wagging lilac tongues, flattened
Fizzling, fading, faint
Purple euphoria ignites
Slumbering queen submerged
In blazing ruby
and sapphire splinters.

Nine bottles
clitter clatter
against honey walnut lips
scented rose water droplets
Trickling, velvet petals
magnolia talc floating
like snowflakes
sinking in showers
Slumbering queen breathing
Failing, Stolen.

Eight plus three
Wild butterflies
trailing restless paths
Thief with a smiling bag
watching, waiting

Slumbering princess shivering
silver tipped crystals
grasping, squeezing
dazzling diamond queen
descending like fairy lights
warm wrinkled kisses
melting, mending, healing.

Seven seals eighteen
Lavender memories
Rose petal reflections
in a red tea house
Lilac embraces and peridot shields
Strawberry ladybirds blush
beside cottonwood trees
Dragonflies flirt
With turquoise reflections
Serene queen, sound asleep
on creamy casablanca stars.

Life Swims

Life swims and ripples around me
shimmering silhouettes dance inside
predators lurk beneath a silken sea of treachery
immersed in reverie of faraway islands
the watery depths of solitary time

My actions and reactions
cast like pebbles
undulating in concentric circles
beyond my control
Life swims and ripples around me

Love letters float within my heart
the flotsam and jetsam of memories
dreams rise and fall in the tide of my footsteps
lesions of life now cicatrices
shimmering silhouettes dance inside

Treading water beneath crashing waves
Sharks and seals, identical, underwater
sandbanks disintegrate between your toes
deep water engulfs without warning
predators lurk beneath a silken sea of treachery

I circle dreams and dreams circle me
lay themselves bare in the sun
a parallel future glints on the horizon
in a place where intention and effort have finally met

immersed in reverie of faraway islands

Learning to swim in the space
between land and sea
Parallel reverie coasts into reality
Evolutionary adventure reflects in
the watery depths of solitary time.

Sycamore Fig

This is the Sycamore Fig
that stages my children's adventures
captures their imagination
ignites their delight
with its finger-painted leaves
its tufts of sprouting fig shoots
and Spinosaurus roots.

I watch them gather fallen twigs
waving them in circles of eight
spidery wands
skimming crevices and collecting
shimmering webs like candyfloss.

Ezra treads, barefooted, over fallen sticky figs
strewn across the earthy grass
Zuri collects caterpillar-eaten leaves
of sepia and autumn green
dropping them in a pile at my feet.

I wonder at the living indentations
that line the wrinkled trunk
the green veins that radiate
beneath skin-coloured bark
tracing my fingers over segments
of cracked bark
shaped like jigsaw pieces
searching the hungry branches

that reach toward the sun-filled, cerulean sky.

We love this majestic old tree
that stands in our adopted garden
filtering the winter sun
dropping caramelized fruit
for bush turkeys that scratch
and scavenge at its feet
the tree that offers hours
of fun and play, inspired writing
and private conversations.

This is the Sycamore Fig
the tree of adventure
where children play and memories make
the tree of inspiration
where adults muse and future plans make
Our tree of life, our tree of love,
Our sycamore fig.

The Death and Life of a Name

My mother used to sew my name tags {Bianca Bowers} inside the collar, seams, and waistbands of my school clothes. My clothes belonged to someone. The proof was stitched into their skin.

My own sense of belonging in South Africa, New Zealand, England and Australia was less tangible. My sense of vocational belonging was even worse; I stumbled from one vapid office job to the next and felt the fists of frustration strengthening as I continued to squander my creative potential.

Belonging, and her doppelgänger identity, remained intangible and continued to manifest negatively until May 2013 - the year that I listened to my heart and waded knee-deep into a reconnaissance mission to locate my belonging and identity in the writing landscape.

For the next 22 months, I hiked up mountains to exercise my voice and hone my style, I crossed terrains in an attempt to identify my weaknesses and strengths, I ran endurance races to test my resolve, and I skinny-dipped in the publishing deep-end.

At some point during my recon I knew that the belonging aspect of my mission was a success. It was as if I had found a name tag stitched into my core: {Writer}
I knew I belonged. There was no question. No denial. No argument. No more proof required. As if my own mother had sewn a name tag into the cloth of my soul at birth.

The writing identity took a little longer... I'm not a person who holds onto things. I frequently jettison the people, habits and sundries that no longer serve me. When I left

South Africa, I left Bianca Bowers behind. She was tainted with abuse, depression and attempted suicide. I was deeply ashamed of her and unwilling to forgive. When I got married 3 years later, I saw the perfect opportunity to change my name and start afresh.

Changing my name turned out to be nothing more than a band aid, and I was soon mourning my discarded identity. Three countries and two children later, I began my writing reconnaissance under the name of B.G. Bowers; a small, albeit, hesitant, step toward reclaiming my birth name and building a writing identity.

There is no doubt that B.G. Bowers and my original bgbowers.com blog have been instrumental in my writing reconnaissance, but, as that mission draws to a close, I recognise that they have served their purpose and accept that it's time to let go. At the start of my mission, I was somewhat preoccupied with building a platform, finding an audience, getting published, and impressing other writers etc. While I certainly wrote a lot, I also scrambled around like a social media butterfly in an attempt to build the pillars of a platform, an audience and publication. Experience has since taught me that pillars are built over time and they have more to do with ones writing portfolio than ones social media activities. While publishing, readership, platforms and marketing are undoubtedly writer-requisites in the 21st Century writing landscape, I now recognise that they play second fiddle to the main event - writing.

The decision to change my author name (from BG Bowers to Bianca Bowers) in 2014 reflects my progress, and bridges the gaps between reconnaissance, belonging and identity. It also signals my contentment to just write. With my second poetry book complete and prepared for publication, I see an explicit path and revolving dimensions of writing maturity flickering on the horizon. I am secure in the knowledge that there are many stories queuing up in my mind. I also acknowledge, accept, and embrace the fact that there are stories that I am not yet skilled enough to tell. I embrace it, because it means learning curves and development and growth - it means that I have a future in writing.

My reconnaissance has come to an end. Like my childhood school clothes, I belong: {Bianca Bowers: Writer}

NOTES

Blue Butterfly
This poem is dedicated to my beloved Art Teacher, from Primary School, who committed suicide.

Dance Me To The End Of Love
This poem references Jack Vettriano's painting Dance Me to the End of Love 1998.

Death and Life I and II
These poems are written using the Palindrome Poetry Form (aka "Mirrored Poetry"), whereby the poem reads the same forward or backward.

Desire
This poem references Gustav Klimt's painting Die Freundinnen 1916

Leaving
This poem was written using the Oulipean method of "larding" (aka "line stretching"), whereby you select several sentences from a chosen text and add new sentences between the selections. The supplementary sentences must either enrich the existing narrative or create a new narrative continuity.
Selected Text: Nervous Conditions, by Tsitsi Dangarembga (Seal Press, 2004)
   Selected sentences (p173):
"I was silent"/ "Nyasha knew nothing about leaving" / "She did not know what essential parts of you stayed behind no matter

how violently you tried to dislodge them in order to take them with you".

Liebe
This poem was written using the Sestina Poetry Form, and is also inspired by the Gustav Klimt painting, *Liebe*.

Life Swims
This poem was written using the Cascade Poetry Form, created by Udit Bhatia, whereby the poem follows the structure a/b/c, d/e/A, f/g/B, h/i/C.

Love Garden
This poem was written in the Vers Beaucoup (many rhymes) poetry form, created by Curt Mongold. Curt contacted me shortly after I posted this on my blog and complimented me on the use of the form. I went on to use his form to write a poem called 'Toxic Release', which was accepted into the Art Toppling Tobacco Project in 2013.

Mortal Girl
This poem is dedicated to Nicole, whose unexpected suicide impacted me greater than I ever could have imagined.

Purple Hibiscus
The title and theme of this poem was inspired by, and makes reference to, Chimamanda Ngozi Adichie's novel, "Purple Hibiscus".

Slumbering Queen

This poem is dedicated to my maternal grandmother, who appeared in spirit form when I attempted suicide and quite possibly saved me.

Smiling Bag
The title of this poem references an episode from the television show Twin Peaks (1991).

The Forgotten Female
This essay was inspired by Sue Monk Kidd's "The Dance of the Dissident Daughter" (HarperOne 1996).

The Kiss
This poem references Gustav Klimt's painting Der Kuss 1907/08

Tree of Life
This poem references Gustav Klimt's central painting Tree of Life within The Stoclet Frieze 1905/6.
This poem was also chosen in 2016 to be featured in a trailer for a short film called *The Avant-Gardener*.

Weekend
This poem is dedicated to Jane, who was killed by a drunk driver on her 18th birthday.

Winter Landscape
This poem is inspired by the painting *Winter Landscape* by Caspar David Friedrich.

About the Author

Bianca Bowers is a South African-born, Australian-based writer who has also lived in the UK and New Zealand. She has authored five poetry books and is currently preparing her novels, *Cape of Storms*, and *Three Hearts* for publication with *Auteur Books*.

She holds a BA in English and Film/TV/Media Studies. In 2016, her poem *Tree of Life* was chosen to feature in a trailer for a short-film called *The Avant-Gardener*. Her poetry has also appeared in *Shot Glass Journal, Tongue In Your Ear*, and *The Art Toppling Tobacco Project*.

You can find Bianca at:
www.biancabowers.com
www.lobby4love.org
www.twitter.com/BB_Writes

A Note From the Author

Thank you for supporting my work.
I upload poetry readings to my YouTube Channel every Friday. To watch the 'Death and Life' Playlist, please subscribe at: https://www.youtube.com/bgbowers

I also offer email subscribers a free PDF version of Pressed Flowers: www.biancabowers.com/subscribe

The publishing landscape has changed. Books live and die by the amount of reviews they receive. Amazon's algorithm, for instance, only kicks in once a book has received 15 reviews of 3 stars and over.
So, dear reader, if you enjoyed this book and wish to help it reach a larger audience, then please consider leaving a review on Amazon and/or Goodreads.
https://amazon.com/author/biancabowers
https://www.goodreads.com/BiancaBowersAuthor

Ugh (how do I write a review?) you might be thinking!

I have included a book review guide on the following page to remove the guesswork. Also, don't be intimidated by length, a review can be as short or long as you wish.

Thank you,

Bianca xo

Book Review Guide

HEADING

YOUR STAR RATING

SUMMARY (OPTIONAL)

EXPLAIN WHAT YOU ENJOYED ABOUT THE BOOK

WHAT WAS YOUR FAVOURITE POEM AND/OR STORY?

DO YOU HAVE A FAVOURITE LINE/QUOTE?

WOULD YOU RECOMMEND THIS BOOK TO SOMEONE? IF SO, WHAT KIND OF READER WOULD THIS APPEAL TO?

LENGTH: A review can be as short or long as you wish.

www.ingramcontent.com/pod-product-compliance
Lightning Source LLC
Chambersburg PA
CBHW070428010526
44118CB00014B/1950